OBJECTS IN THE ASHMOLEAN

AN ART AND POETRY RESOURCE

DIANA MOORE

First published in 2017

© Diana Moore, 2017

All images (except Greater Flamingo) © Ashmolean Museum, University of Oxford

Greater Flamingo © Bodleian Libraries, University of Oxford

Cover design and interior layout: possage.com

ISBN 978-1-5442-9477-3

OBJECTS IN THE ASHMOLEAN

An art and poetry resource for reading and performance

The Ashmolean Museum is the world's first purpose-built public museum. It holds a remarkably diverse collection of objects dating from 8000 BC to the present day. These poems tell the story of a special few that caught my eye. When I researched their backgrounds, I found that they all had wonderful stories to tell.

In this book you can journey from Renaissance Italy to the Far East; you can time travel between ancient artefacts and works of modern art. This book will serve as a valuable learning resource for some readers; for others, it is a little gallery of its own. Each poem begins with a short introduction letting you know some of the fascinating history of the object that inspired it.

Many of these poems are well suited to live performance; each one has been performed at the Ashmolean in its relevant gallery. You'll find pieces in here that can be set to music or acted out. Occasionally, I'll give you a clue about a tune or a rhythm you can try. There is drama, humour, song - and one poem can even be used as a prompt for meditation! I hope these poems will engage and inspire you and lead you to try out even more ideas.

All these wonderful objects sit silently in the halls of the Ashmolean. How will you bring them to life?

Please note, it is possible from time to time that some of the objects may be absent (on loan or in storage), but you can ask about their location.

Enlightened...?

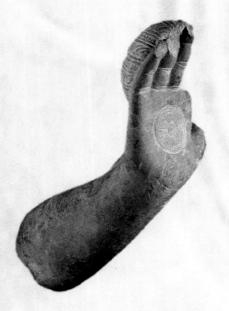

A hand of Buddha reaches out to us, in blessing. On its palm we find the Wheel of Dharma, a motif that represents the Buddha's teachings. Looking at a fragment such as this, and, imagining the once far-larger statue from which it came, we might meditate upon what ancient teachings mean for us today.

ⓘ *Fragmentary forearm and hand from the Buddha, 2nd Century AD (101 - 200)*

🎨 *Pink sandstone*

📍 *Ground floor, Room 12, India to 600*

🏷️ *Accession number EA1997.186*

And I am searching
Yet
Losing my way

You have reminded me
to practise
Practise calm
Every day

So
I went out seeking
And stopped
Still....

Breathing in
a purifying breath
Quelling the fidgety form
To submission

* ✳ *

And the little boy
came to me
Wearing a hat of yellow brocade
A golden temple
on his head

He smiled
One of his lives
At me

And here you are to remind me
You who have stood centuries
And stood for what?

You elude me
Then you come and bring your light
And I want to be where the light is

Two Bream and a Ray

This plate was made some time around 400 BC but has managed to survive for over 2000 years in one piece. Although you'll find it in the Rome gallery, it is Greek in design. Perhaps it would have sat well on the dining table of the poet Archestratus. Archestratus was from Sicily and spent his life travelling the Mediterranean, writing about food, particularly fish. He even wrote a book called Hedypathia, or 'The Life of Luxury', about his gastronomic adventures. Cast your eye over this menu of gourmet fish poems and see what takes your fancy.

🛈 *Red-figure pottery plate for serving fish: Two sea bream and a ray. Campanian, 4th Century BC (400 - 301). From Cumae.*

🎨 *Ceramic*

📍 *Ground floor, Gallery 13, Rome 400BC - AD300*

🏷 *Accession number AN1872.1243.b*

Archestratus, by the shore with a basket of fish:

Two bream and a ray
Two bream and a ray
Anybody...?
Lovely fish

Look at this, fresh from Ephesus
Beautiful gilt-head bream
What a dream little catch eh?
Well not so little
It's a good 10 cubits

And here's a nice bit of ray
Not the catch of the day
But you can boil it
Add a drop of oil to it
The yellow-grey stuff – and add a few green leaves

I know my fish
I know all the best places to find them, buy them
Prepare and cook 'em.

The name is
Archestratus
Poet and gourmet guide
From Gela, Sicily
330 BC
Give or take a century

Come and dine with me
Nouvelle cuisine is my forte

And I have a little fun along the way
In parody

"Pythagoras, Diodorus
Come and try this lovely fish!"

Let's take a look at the menu

9

TWO BREAM AND A RAY

Cumae   *Bay of Naples*

Favourites

The boar-fish is first rate in Tarentum
And baked tuna tail from Byzantium
Dipped in a sharp brine
All mine

(No sharing platters if I can help it)

Appetizers

Bream - Cooked two ways
Could this be my dream food..?

Stars shining bright above me...
Dream a little.. steam a little.. bream for me

If you're going to take it serious
You have to look to Sirius
And see where it positions in the sky
Rising up in Delos
By the fair-harboured houses
Of the brine
You can eat the head and tail
In a yellow-grey oil

Just buy the head and tail
Don't bother with the rest
It's past its best

But listen to this:
Do not pass by the fat gilt-head from Ephesus
Get one of those babes of holy Selinus
Wash it properly, bake it and serve it whole
Even if it is 10 cubits long

You shall have a fishy
On a little dishy....

Mid-winter warmers

BOILED RAY SEASONED WITH SILPHIUM

"Daddy… what's silphium?"

"Well son it's a yellow flower used as a seasoning - to make your food taste nice – and it is used in medicine.. how about that! You learn something new every day, son."

ELECTRIC RAY BOILED IN OIL, WINE, FRAGRANT LEAVES AND A LITTLE GRATING OF CHEESE

You shall have a fishy
On a little dishy
You shall have…

A lobster from Lipari
Parrotfish from Chalcedon
Prawns from Macedonia and Ambracia

And in the city of Torone
You must buy the one and only
Dog shark belly
The very underbelly
Of the dog-shark belly
Dog-shark shark
Underbelly .. underbelly
Sublime…Mmm…divine

Sprinkle with cumin
Bake with a little salt
Add a little yellow-grey oil

We haven't yet invented foil…

Bake this delicacy
Dog-shark underbelly

Add your pounded sauce
And trimmings
Sweetest, luxurious meat

Special of the Day

EELS EELS AND MORE EELS

Let us praise the eel
With the most appeal
The conger and the moray
Eels
My favourite meals
Are eels

So…

[The following can be sung to the tune of Dean Martin's That's Amore]

When you hear someone squeal
Cos they just saw an eel
That's a moray

Kiddies menu

[To the tune of Frère Jacques]

Archestratus
What's for starters?
Sea bream stew
Boiled ray too
Dress it up with silphium
Put a little salt in
Fragrant leaves
Grated cheese

What shall I choose?
Two bream and a ray?
Two bream and a ray
Anyone?

Henry VIII and His Six Wives

Here is a face that most of us can recognise, and a stern looking face it is too. By the time this bust was carved in the early seventeenth century, Henry VIII was long since dead. Henry's legacy lived on: his patronage of the arts, his reformation of the church, and, most notoriously of all, his string of marriages. What follows is a poetic script for performance.

ⓘ *Bust of Henry VIII, early 17th century*

🎨 *Marble*

📍 *Second floor, Room 41, England 400 - 1600*

🏷️ *Accession number AN1896-1908 G.1228*

Narrator: Here we have the marble bust of Henry VIII, looking very pale compared to his colourful character and he still elicits strong feelings more than 500 years after his accession to the throne.

Henry ruled for thirty eight years and was married to Katherine of Aragon for 23 years. He was driven by his need for a male heir to succeed him, so he broke from the Catholic Church and married five more times.

Today we're going to be hearing from Henry and his wives. Henry was keen to write some contemporary lines, and we've managed to reach him using a mobile app... it's called 'Ghost App' ... you can find it at woooooo.com ... so, let's go to the app and meet the Tudor King.

Henry, what do you have say to Katherine of Aragon – she's still very keen to be your wife?

Henry: *(Thoughtfully)* Katherine of Aragon . . . Oh! Yes!
Hi Kate
No more dates!
How about a change of title, eh?
Princess Dowager? Princess Dowager?
How would ya, how would ya like to be . . ?

Katherine of Aragon: No I don't like it
No I won't take it
The title that is vital to me
You see... is
Mrs Henry Tudor
Mrs! Mrs! Mrs!
I'm your Queen not a princess

Henry: And I need an heir to the throne - where is Cardinal Wolsey? I have to get a divorce.

K of A: And I don't like that woman. *[Exit KATHERINE OF ARAGON]*

Henry: She means Lady Anne Boleyn. . . and I do . . . I do! *[Enter ANNE BOLEYN]*

Anne Boleyn:	Henry?
Henry:	Anne, my love, you look glamorous . . . let me nearer, I feel amorous!
AB:	Henry darling, not tonight Make me queen... and then I might
Henry:	You have my jewels, you have my heart, Is it not time we made a start? [Circle chase]
AB:	I take your heart I take your jewels I won't be taken for a fool
	Needs must, and I must be wary Look how you dumped my sister Mary Now go and get a divorce from the Pope and marry me! [Exit HENRY, frustrated]
	(To audience) I'm not going to be like my younger sister She ended up with nothing Henry used and dismissed her I want to rule the land, yeah I want to be queen If I don't get what I want I'll scream and scream. *[Exit ANNE BOLEYN,* *Enter KATHERINE OF ARAGON]*
K of A:	And another thing Henry... where are you?
Henry:	Yes, what now? 23 years of marriage . . . no boys . . . No heirs, no spares...
K of A:	My nephew Charles is in a temper He's the Holy Roman Emperor Divorce, says he, is not permitted

Catholics just don't allow it
You really have to be committed
For life, life, life
I am your wife
And marriage laws are marriage laws
I pray there is no get out clause
Oh! Henry...

Henry: What?

K of A: I love you

Henry: Goodbye Katarina   [Exit KATHERINE OF ARAGON]
Hellooo Queen Anne Boleyn!   [Enter ANNE BOLEYN, to wedding march – they kiss]
Mwa, mwa!

AB: *(Nervous)* Hi Henry...
It's a girl

Henry: I don't like girls as much as boys.
It's taken seven years
To get here
And for what reason?
I'm tiring of her tantrums . . .
Time for a little treason
Goodbye Anne!

AB: My crown, my name
I have been framed...
Byyyyyyyye   [Exit ANNE BOLEYN]
                                                          [Enter ghost of JANE SEYMOUR]

Henry: Ah! Jane, sweet Jane, from lady-in-waiting to lady-awaiting . . .
Tick, tock, tick, tock,

Henry: Seven months, eight months, nine months –
A boy!   An heir!
My son
But you're not here!

Narrator: Wife number 4, calling wife number 4
A cameo of Anne of Cleves, by Hans Holbein

[Enter ANNE OF CLEVES horse-like, clip clopping, neighing]

Anne of Cleves: Your majesty!

Henry: Oh! No! No! No! This cameo is misleading
With her, I'll not be breeding.

[ANNE OF CLEVES neighs, snuffles, backs off, exits]

I have no care
For a *Flanders Mare*!
I've been put on the spot
And I like her not!

Narrator: Call for the young and nubile Katherine Howard!

Katherine Howard: Your majesty
Oh! Great!
He's overweight
Need a peg Ooh!
Gammy leg Ooh!
But wait...
I can be queen
Love the gifts
The shifts
Beautiful material
Shimmering   ethereal
As long as I am not seen

[dancing towards HENRY]

	Cavorting and courting	*[dances]*
	Yoo-hoo Mr Culpepper	
	Oh! Dear... caught out...	

Henry: Goodbye, young Katherine.

[Exit KATHERINE HOWARD]
[Enter CATHERINE PARR]

Catherine Parr: Tra la la la laaaaaaa
I am Catherine Parr

[pause, HENRY coughs]

There, there Henry

Henry: Oh! My leg . . . my bones . . . my head . . .
Am I dead?

CP: There, there, Henry

Henry: Do I have a little time
For one last rhyme?

CP: Not Greensleeves?   *[She checks HENRY'S forehead]*
Go ahead

Henry: I want a girl named Mary Lou
So I can write a clerihew
Instead I wed: one Jane, two Annes, three Kates
Wish I had time . . . for a few more dates . . .   *[HENRY expires]*

CP: I have nursed an aging king
Now he's dead
I can sing:

(Sings as in Greensleeves) For I have kept my head in place
I have outlived his noble Grace

I've Got the Silver-Finned Blues

This magical image is part of an Italian renaissance altarpiece. It is a painting full of contrasts: danger and safety, good and evil, darkness and light. St Nicholas arrives in a blaze of stars to save the sailors from the storm - but who is that we glimpse in the bottom left corner? Mermaids have often been depicted as allegories of temptation and sin. Yet this one is fleeing, not into the shadowy side of the picture, but into the light. Perhaps this mermaid has been misunderstood. What is she thinking? Is she afraid? Was she coming to help the sailors? Could it be that this story of heroes and villains is not so simple after all?

ⓘ *Bicci di Lorenzo, St Nicholas of Bari Banishing the Storm, 1433 - 35*

🎨 *Tempera and gilding on panel*

📍 *Second floor, Gallery 42, Early Italian art*

🏷 *Accession number WA1850.26*

I've got the silver-finned blues
I've been painted by a muse
They've labelled me as pagan
I might as well be Satan
For every time I sing sublimely
I get accused

Of stirring up a storm
When all I want to do is warn

When I see waves a-lashing (lashing)
Masts come down a-crashing (crashing)

I could make a sailor cosy
Take him to my shell abode-y
Down, deep under the sea
But how can I lose
My silver-finned blues..?

Here comes Father Nicholas
Saviour of the day
He is kind and generous
He wants me out the way…?

If… I offer him oysters
In the cloisters
Sing to the wind
After we've… 'sinned'

Pray for his so-o-o-oul

St Nick, St Nick, St Nicholas, St Nicholas
Grant this fish
This human fish
A wish
Splish! Splish!

For, how am I to form a bond..?
One sprinkle from your starry wand….

What! No?
He says go!
Well that's not very generous
St Nicholas

Help me!   Help me!

I am gone
I must swim on… on… on….

And I feel

Bicci di Lorenzo
We are no longer friends so
I think I'll find a different ship
I'm on my way, I've had a tip

I must say 'bye-bye'
No tear in my eye

But that's why
I've got the silver-finned blues

Pan and his Pipes

Pan, the shepherd-god of ancient Greece, is holding up his famous reedy pipes. The name of this little bronze sculpture tells us whose voice he is playing along with: 'Pan listening to Echo'. There are many versions of this myth, but here Pan is shown in a more human form, with feet instead of cloven hooves. The following is an echo poem with a musical feel; how will you conjure up the voices of Pan and his invisible love?

- ❗ *Pan Listening to Echo, Inkstand, 1530 - 40, perhaps made by Desiderio da Firenze, (active Veneto 1532 - 45), Padua, about 1530 - 40*
- 🎨 *Copper alloy with silvering in eyes*
- 💧 *Second floor, Gallery 43, Italian Renaissance*
- 🏷️ *Accession number WA1899.CDEF.B1077*

Pan and his pipes. Pan and his pipes. Pipes, pipes, pipes.
Pan and his pipes. Pan and his pipes. Pipes, pipes, pipes.
He's stopped and he's stopped in his tracks. Tracks.
What is it in the air that he lacks? Lacks, lacks.

I have waited in the meadow with the flowers. Hours.
Sweet are the meadowsweet and cowslip. Slip.
Here in the meadow, alone by and by
I sigh. Sigh.

Where are you Echo my love? I Love.
You are my only love. Am I your only one? Only one.
Here am I for you always, to no other will I go. Go.
Is that you singing in the leaves? Don't leave me. Leave me.
Alone, I don't want to be alone. Alone.

What say you plants...?
Come Crested Dogs-Tail. I ail. Ail.
Do you feel low, as I do, Musk Mallow? Low.
Are you ill for love, Tormentil? Ill.

Here among the meadow brome. I roam
I roam and seek your presence. Essence.
I have waited in the meadow, sweet meadow. Oh!
Echo, come take my hand. And
I will wait for you here in the meadow. Oh! Woe!

A Time to Bond

The face of this baby boy is full of wisdom. He tilts his head upwards to regard his mother, stiller by far than a real life infant or toddler. Perhaps the pair can hear the distant sounds of St Mark's Square that we can see through the window behind them. This is 'The Virgin and Child with a View of Venice' or the 'Tallard Madonna', a tender version of a familiar scene. The following poem imagines the individual thoughts of this most remarkable mother and child, in an early moment of peace such as that shown in the painting.

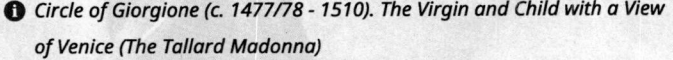

ⓘ *Circle of Giorgione (c. 1477/78 - 1510). The Virgin and Child with a View of Venice (The Tallard Madonna)*

🎨 *Second floor, Gallery 43, Italian Renaissance*

📍 *Oil on panel*

🏷️ *Accession number WA1949.222*

Chant

(Sing softly)

Feeding Healing   *Feeding Healing*
Teaching Praying   *Teaching Praying*

Feed - ing   Heal - ing   Teach - ing   Pray - ing

Child

Chant
(Sing softly)

Feeding Healing
Teaching Praying

Feeding Healing
Teaching Praying

Oh! Mummy… read me the story of the
five loaves and two fishes again… again…

Let's go to Galilee
Galilee
Over the sea

And what's for tea?

Fish and bread
Make it spread

Water to wine
Miracle time

Cast your net
Don't forget

Believe believe in me
In Gali-Galilee

Mummy… we can be playful
Yet a little while…
For then I must be about my Father's business

Breaking bread
Breaking bread
Who is risen
From the dead?

Mother

Child,
My soul rests in you
My heart blessed in you
My wound dressed in you

Oh! little lamb
Come along
Sweet serene boy
Bringer of joy

And yes…
Let us go to Galilee
Galilee
Over the sea…

My soul rests in you
My heart blessed in you
My wound dressed in you

I watch, I pray, I say
My child
This is my child
Do not betray

Oh! Lord have mercy
Lord have mercy

Come along
Sweet serene boy
Bringer of joy
Oh! little lamb

Feeding Healing
Teaching Praying

My soul rests in you
My heart blessed in you
My wound dressed in you

Feeding Healing
Teaching Praying

My soul rests in you….

Breaking bread
Breaking bread

He is risen
From the dead

29

Heaven or Hell...?

Heaven is triumphant! St Michael vanquishes the devil! And yet... surely our eyes cannot help but be drawn to that fearful gaping mouth below. Through the gates of hell, the human figures are in chaos, abandoned to their horrid tumble. Do we empathise with Satan? Does he share the sinners' plight? You can have fun dancing with the devil in this next poem, which can be sung, in part, to the tune of Offenbach's 'Infernal Galop', popularly called the Can Can.

ⓘ *Lelio Orsi, St Michael subduing Satan and weighing the Souls of the Dead,*
   c. 1540 - 49
🎨 *Oil on panel*
📍 *Second floor, Gallery 43, Italian Renaissance*
🏷 *Accession number WA1960.70*

< drums > **Introduction**

< chorus > **See the people in a jumble**
How they fall and how they tumble
Crumbling beneath the rocks
Beneath the ground
In Satan's mouth
< slow up > **There's no way out...**

Satan - have we got a date on?
Satan - have we got a date on?

Aaaah! Aaaagh!
Satan's mouth
No way out
Aaaah! Aaaagh!

Stumbling in isolation
Void of clear communication
Is your heart filled with damnation
What is your soul's revelation?

- -

Are you in heaven?
Are you in hell?
What are your thoughts in this minute, do tell?

Are you suffering in circles?
Do you have a secret fear?
What will make you change your actions
If you think you'll end up here?

31

Have you diddled your expenses?
Did you steal your best friend's bride?
Have you sworn on oath and lied?
Are you over-filled with pride?

Like
Lucifer
Fallen Star
Angels, Angels
Lucifer
Fallen Star
Angels, Angels

< higher note, now optimistic >

Angels, Angels, Angels, Angels, Angels, Angels

< to the tune of
Offenbach's Infernal Galop >
(Can Can)

Do not dice with paradise
Or you will end up in a hole
Run by Satan with a weight upon your sad and wretched soul , so...
Do your praying
Ask for healing
Clear your sins
And cleanse your soul
Up the ante
Follow Dante
Go beyond the inferno

Angels ! Angels!
Come and rescue me from hell
Angels! Angels!
I will learn my lessons well

Angels ! Angels!
Show me how to be divine
Angels! Angels!
Take me with you to cloud nine

Michael listen to St Michael when he quotes Isaiah
Listen to him when he says you can't be higher
Michael listen to St Michael, end this evil cycle
Do not try to step out of your line

How far have you fallen?
Is it lust or greed or heresy ?
Avarice or cowardice or violence wrath or treachery and...
Is the crime a heavy burden ?
Do you plan to mend your ways?
Major, minor misdemeanours
Steer well clear avoid the blaze

Angels! Angels!
Come and rescue me from hell
Angels! Angels!
I will learn my lessons well

Angels! Angels!
Show me how to be divine
Angels! Angels!
Take me with you to cloud nine cloud nine cloud nine cloud nine

Drums

Finale

Is there Still Life with a Lobster and Turkey...?

Of all the paintings to end up in, this lobster and turkey have found themselves inside a still life. Despite the extraordinary detail with which Abraham van Beyeren has drawn this sumptuous spread, still lifes were ranked below other genres of painting in the seventeenth century. They are still somewhat overlooked today. Perhaps the objects in the picture are similarly unimpressed and are wishing that they were somewhere else. Perhaps if we were to lean in closer we could overhear their conversation...

ℹ️ *Abraham van Beyeren - Still Life with a Lobster and Turkey, c. 1653*

🎨 *Oil on canvas*

📍 *Second floor, Still-life paintings*

🏷️ *Accession number WA1940.2.11*

This poem can be performed to the tune of Amilcare Ponchielli – Dance of the Hours

(More popularly known as 'Hello Mudder, Hello Fadder')

Said the lobster   to the turkey
How I find this   canvas murky
Shall we go out   in the sunshine
And perhaps I can locate an ocean with brine

Said the turkey   let us walk now
Though I find it   hard to talk now
It is one of   my endeavours
To retrieve my head and neck and coat of feathers

Are you leaving?   Asked the melon
Would you want to   be a felon?
Not at all dear   squealed the lemon
It's appealing to be free so don't condemn them

Help me off this platter lobster
Help me off this platter lobster
I am stuck   I think I'm out of luck
Unless you load me on a truck   What luck!   What luck!

As they set off   down a pathway
They were met by   someone half way
It was eerie   *misterioso*
They had bumped into the ghost of Caravaggio

Said the artist   May I paint you
And I promise   Not to taint you
But the lobster   Cried 'Let's scurry!
I would rather be a telephone by Dali!'

35

Flamingo Calypso

This elegant flamingo was commissioned by Lady Mary Impey as part of her late eighteenth century collection of Indian bird paintings. Of all the exotic birds she saw in her time abroad, which better to celebrate than the flamingo with its lovely S-shaped neck and delicate colours? The following poem can be devised and set to a calypso-style tune.

🛈 *Shaikh Zain ud-Din, Greater Flamingo (Phoenicopteros ruber), 1781*
🎨 *Gouache on paper*
📍 *Eastern Art Paintings, Jameel Centre*
🏷 *Accession number LI901.18*
© *Bodleian Libraries, University of Oxford*

Flamingo
Flamingo
Calypso
Calypso

Oh! Flingo
Your wingo
Let's go go
Let's go go

Slow ... slow
Quick quick slow
Slow ... slow
Quick quick slow

Oh! Flingo
Your wingo
Flamingo
Flamingo

In a ringo
Sing-a-lingo
Flamingo
Flamingo   [Repeat]

Lift your pink toe
Only one though   [Add a nod of head]
Flamingo
Flamingo   [Repeat]

And so so
We know know
Flamingo
Calypso

We know know
we know know
Flamingo
Calypso

Gilbert Cannan and his Mill

This is a painting full of hidden triangles. The man we can see is Gilbert Cannan, the early twentieth century author. With him are two dogs, one of which belonged to his friend J.M. Barrie, and if you know Peter Pan you'll recognise the black and white dog as Nana, the Darling children's nurse. The friendship collapsed when Barrie's wife Mary divorced him and married Cannan, with whom she'd been having an affair. The man who painted Cannan had an even more tempestuous private life. Mark Gertler had been so passionately in love with the artist, Dora Carrington, that he threatened to kill himself when he heard of her marriage to Ralph Partridge. Dora, in turn, had been unrequited in her love for the author Lytton Strachey. The real life triangles were, it seems, as colourful as those in the picture itself.

ⓘ *Mark Gertler - Gilbert Cannan and his Mill, c. 1916*

🎨 *Oil on canvas*

📍 *Third floor, Gallery 62, Modern art*

🏷️ *Accession number WA1968.24*

What's in a triangle?
Who's in a triangle?
Where are the triangles?
One   two three

A conical mill
A conical tree
Triangular man
With his legs in a 'V'

Triangles
Triangles
Do you love triangles
Do you love   art lovers
Do   Do you?

Gilbert Cannan
The man in the frame
A lawyer and writer
Where did he find fame?

In triangles triangles
One   two   three

Gilbert …Mary … JM Barrie

Gilbert met Mary
Who was married to Barrie
Author of Neverland's Peter Pan
Can you see how the dog on the right
Looks like Nan..
Nana Nana   Cannan and Nana
And Mary together
The dog was devoted and voted to be-
long to Mary   one   two three

Triangles   Triangles
Triangles

The painter is Gertler
Who started out poor
Connected with Gilbert
And artists galore

Mark… Dora… Gilbert

Mark wanted Dora
Dora loved *Lytton*
Gilbert and Mark were artistically smitten
In triangles
Angular
Triangles
Tangle of triangles
A-cute-ness   of   triangles

Gilbert… Gwen… Henry…

Here is a story
Of   polyamory   poly-amoré

Gilbert loved Gwen
(He'd moved on from Mary)
Henry the lodger
One   two   three
Un   deux   trois

Here in this art
Poplars like   pampas grass
Do you hear whisperings
Scandalous sculptures
And
Triangles Triangles
One   two three

Gilbert was busy
While Henry and Gwen
Too busy to see
How the two sides   went
So   well   together
Two gather in marriage

From equilateral
To isolated angle
Of a triangle
Gilbert was sad   eventually   mad

There's a conical Mill
And a conical tree
A triangular man with his legs in a 'V'

What's in a triangle?
Who's in a triangle?
Where are the triangles?

One   two   three

Bibliography

Wilkins, John and Shaun Hill. 'Archestratus: Fragments from The Life of Luxury'. Devon: Prospect Books, 2011.

Biography

Diana Moore is a poet, performer, playwright, and author of: *A Fishy Coat Tale and Other Poems*, and *A Visitor to the Forest*, a performance poem/ensemble piece inspired by Paolo Uccello's painting of 'The Hunt in the Forest' which hangs in the Ashmolean Museum.

Diana inspires and educates both children and adults using visual art in live performances. She devises creative writing and poetry performance workshops which she runs for all ages. Venues include: schools, theatres, residential homes and museums.

Diana is a regular contributor to the 'Poetry Tours in the Galleries', and the more recent 'Ekphrasis Poetry' at the Ashmolean Museum.

If you have any questions or comments, or if you would like to enquire about a visit to your establishment, please email: diana@diana-moore.com.

84993970R00027

Made in the USA
Lexington, KY
28 March 2018